FOCUSED LEADERSHIP

What You Can Do Today To Become A More Effective Leader

Ervin (Earl) Cobb

ALSO BY

ERVIN (EARL) COBB

The Leadership Advantage
Do More. Lead More. Earn More.

Pillow Talk Consciousness
Intimate Reflections on America's 100 Most Interesting
Thoughts and Suspicions

God's Goodness & Our Mindfulness
Responding Versus Reacting to Life Changing Circumstances

Living a Richer Life
Getting the Most out of Life's Gifts and Circumstances

Navigating the Life Enrichment Model™

Copyright © 2011 by Richer Life, LLC

Published and distributed by ╪RICHER Press
An Imprint of Richer Life, LLC

4600 E. Washington Street, Suite 300, Phoenix, Arizona 85034
www.richerlifellc.com

Cover Design: Richer Media USA
Photographs: Richer Media USA and Big Stock Photo

No part of this publication may be reproduced, stored in a retrieval system, or transmitted in any form or by any means, electronic, mechanical, photocopying, recording, scanning, or otherwise, except as permitted under Section 107 or 108 of the 1976 United States Copyright Act, without prior written permission of the publisher.

RICHER Publications books and products are available through most bookstores. RICHER Publications also publishes its books in a variety of electronic formats. Some content that appears in print may not be available in electronic books.

Library of Congress Cataloging-in-Publications Data

Cobb, Ervin (Earl)
Focused Leadership: What You Can Do Today to Become a More Effective Leader
Ervin (Earl) Cobb -- 1st edition
p.   cm.
ISBN 978-0-9744617-5-5 (hbk : alk. Paper)
1. Management 2. Leadership 3. Reference

2011919726

ISBN 13: 978-0-9744617-6-2

ISBN 10: 09744617-62

Text set is Adobe Garamond
First edition, November 2011

Printed in the United States of America

╬RICHER Press
An Imprint of Richer Life, LLC

RICHER Press is a full service, specialty Trade publisher whose sole goal is to *shape thoughts and change lives for the better*. All of the books, eBooks and digital media we publish, distribute and market embrace our commitment to help maximize opportunities for personal growth and professional achievement.

To learn more visit
www.richerlifellc.com.

ACKNOWLEDGEMENTS

Thanks to all of the mentors, colleagues, co-workers and friends with whom I have had the opportunity to work with, learn from and lead over the past thirty-five years.

Also, special thanks to my wife and soul mate, Charlotte, for her support, her encouragement and for allowing me to spend so much time alone in order to complete this book.

CONTENTS

Preface	9
Introduction	11
Chapter One: Preparing Yourself to Focus	17
"First Classified DoD Space Shuttle Mission"	21
Step-1 Lead with Intention, Not Authority	29
Step-2 Envision the End at the Start	33
Chapter Two: Preparing Your Team to Win	37
"Rescuing Scott O'Grady"	43
Step-3 Articulate Your Vision, Repeatedly	47
Chapter Three: Setting Tactical Parameters	51
"Leading Change During Times of Unchartered Circumstance"	57
Step-4 Don't Allow Bumps in the Road to Distract You	71
Step 5 Energize Others to Do Their Best	75
Step-6 Remember, it's Not All About You	79

Chapter Four: Setting Strategic Parameters   83

"When a Whisper is a Roar"   87

Step-7 Set a Course Lined with Short-term Successes   95

Step-8 Have the Courage to Make the Right Decisions   99

Step-9 Insist on Accountability and Respect from All   103

Chapter Five: Leading and Winning   107

"In the Eye of a Hurricane"   111

Step-10 Persist with Purpose, Passion and Focus   119

Author's Note   123

About the Author   125

PREFACE

FOCUSED LEADERSHIP is not your typical leadership book.

MOST BOOKS on leadership do a fine job presenting leadership concepts, principles, processes, styles, character attributes, methods and current trends. *Focused Leadership* correspondingly incorporates many of these classical and foundational perspectives within the context of its brief and concise discussions on leading and winning. However, *Focused Leadership* is much more than your typical leadership book.

I have written *Focused Leadership* to first be a small book filled with stimulating and inspiring personal anecdotes about my own leadership experiences. I have included stories which epitomize the leadership approach that I shaped, refined and used to get the leadership results I have desired over the years. This approach is now referred to as the "10-Step Approach to Leading and Winning."

In addition, I have thoughtfully filled *Focused Leadership* with some *straight talk* and experience-based ideas as to *"what you can do"* to become a more effective leader today.

Just as importantly, I have also included my qualified perspective on *"what you will gain"* and *"what you will avoid"* if you choose to integrate some of these modest, yet powerful, ideas into your present leadership approach.

All of the ideas I have incorporated into *Focused Leadership* have been personally *tested* and *refined* over the years within nationally recognized and highly respected small, mid-size and Fortune 100 companies as well as in non-profit and civic settings.

I have thoroughly enjoyed being a student of leadership for over three decades. I have similarly enjoyed my role as an adjunct professor of leadership and organizational behavior. I feel very fortunate to have had the opportunity to lead organizations in numerous industries ranging from computers to banking, from wireless communications to aerospace electronics and from pharmaceutical supply chain management to information technology.

Irrespective of your current organization and whether you are new to leadership development or a veteran leader, I strongly believe that you will find *Focused Leadership* filled with practical and valuable ideas that you can use today to lead and to win.

Ervin (Earl) Cobb
Phoenix, Arizona

INTRODUCTION

"Great leadership is about human experiences, not processes. Leadership is not a formula or a program, it is a human activity that comes from the heart and considers the hearts of others. It is an attitude, not a routine." --- Lance Secretan

IN MAY OF 2008, I experienced something for the first time in my thirty-year professional career. I was told by the Wells Fargo Bank, after its acquisition of Wachovia, that there was *"no room for me at the Inn."*

I joined Wells Fargo's technology group following my move back to Phoenix in 2006. My return to Phoenix concluded a chapter in my career that started when I left Phoenix, and Motorola, in 1997 to accept the position of Vice President of Operations with the Reynolds and Reynolds Company in Dayton, Ohio.

During the decade following the move to Dayton, I experienced what many corporate managers and executives experienced during this period. The explosion of the Internet culture; the threat of Y2K; the rise & fall of the dot-com era; the recession of the late 1990's; the financial and economic fall-out of 9/11; and the expansion of the infamous U.S. housing bubble.

Thanks to the forces at work during this era, I was fortunate to hold a number of corporate positions with leadership titles. They included Vice President of Operations, Corporate Vice President of Enterprise Process Development, Chief Operating Officer and Chief Executive Officer.

However, it wasn't until after being released by Wells Fargo, just after being promoted to the position of Head of Data Center Management, that I added the title of "author."

Prior to the Wells Fargo Bank episode, I had enjoyed the option that all successful senior managers and corporate executives cherish --- being able to stay with or leave a company at your own choosing. But, the Great Recession of 2007/2009 changed this American way of life for tens of millions of Americans.

After deciding to take a short "breather" and some precious time to decide what was next, I began to do something that I have always enjoyed but had not found the time to do very much of --- thinking and writing about the things in life that motivate and encourage others. During this time, along with my wife, I completed and published my first two books.

The first book was a combination of a real-life story about self-discovery and how we arrived at our present "view of life" as well as a pseudo memoir titled, *Living a Richer Life: Getting the Most out of Life's Gifts and Circumstances*. The second book turned out to be a captivating story about the social and political discourse which frames the lives and conversations of average Americans at this nexus of the 21st century titled, *Pillow Talk Consciousness: Intimate Reflections on America's 100 Most Interesting Thoughts and Suspicions*.

Following this refreshing and rewarding leap into the world of authorship, I began to spend more time reflecting on my career as a technologist, corporate executive and entrepreneur. I first had to confess to myself that this exercise was as much an attempt to appraise my present inner health as it was a walk through my past.

The disappointing experience I had with the Wells Fargo Bank was still a conundrum. However, I was somewhat surprised by just how many great stories I could vividly recall involving the dozens of teams I have led and the roaring successes that catapulted me to decades of awards, recognitions and six-figure paydays. The most memorable anecdotes, covering the three decades, involved hundreds of team members, co-workers and mentors who not only brought everything to life but were responsible for much of the success and all the lessons learned.

It was this period of reflection, along with the encouragement of my wife, that led to me decide to more fully document my management career and leadership philosophy. I have long been a student of leadership and thoroughly enjoyed the work which gave rise to this book, *Focused Leadership: What I Can Do Today to Become a More Effective Leader.*

Unlike most books on the subject of leadership that primarily discuss concepts, principles and styles, *Focused Leadership* sets forth an array of plausible ideas that can be acted upon today to help you become a more effective leader. Along with the ideas, I also share some experience-based "straight talk" which details *"what you will gain"* and *"what you will avoid"* by taking such action.

Focused Leadership is a book which serves two main purposes.

The first is to give me the opportunity to share with you five of the dozens of anecdotes I documented as a way to recall a few of the memorable moments I have encountered and the valuable lessons I have learned during my career.

The second is to provide you a synopsis of the approach I diligently crafted, refined and applied in order to get the leadership results I desired. I have thoughtfully incorporated a series of informative and concise discussions regarding this approach, which I now call the "10-Step Approach to Leading and Winning", throughout the five chapters of the book.

It is my hope that you will enjoy reading the anecdotes and assessing my approach to leading and winning. The goal is for you to find value in keeping this book nearby and available for those times when you are facing new leadership challenges. If you occasionally find a "nugget" or two that you can take away and add to your cadre of leadership skills and experiences, *Focused Leadership* will have met all of my expectations.

FOCUSED LEADERSHIP
10-Step Approach to Leading and Winning

1. **L**ead with Intention, Not Authority.
2. **E**nvision the End at the Start.
3. **A**rticulate Your Vision, Repeatedly.
4. **D**on't Allow Bumps in the Road to Distract You.
5. **E**nergize Others to Do Their Best.
6. **R**emember, it's Not All About You.
7. **S**et a Course Lined with Short-term Success.
8. **H**ave the Courage to Make the Right Decisions.
9. **I**nsist on Accountability and Respect from All.
10. **P**ersist with Purpose, Passion and Focus.

CHAPTER ONE

PREPARING YOURSELF TO FOCUS

"By failing to prepare you are preparing to fail."

---Benjamin Franklin

PREPARING YOURSELF TO FOCUS

IF I COULD ASK all of the world class athletes on earth what is the one thing that is essential to being in position to win at any level of competition, chances are they all unanimously would say "preparation." Preparing yourself to be in a position to focus your attention and thought on the plans, strategy and passion required to successfully lead an organization is a fundamental element of *Focused Leadership*.

Preparation is generally defined as the action of making something ready for some occasion, test or duty. However, throughout my career, I have always regarded preparation as essential to doing my very best. In addition, I have also been of the mindset that preparation is not a single action but a process.

Unlike a single action, a process is marked by measured changes that lead toward a particular result. Of course, the result I always expect is to succeed at every leadership task I undertake. Not from an arrogant perspective, but from a belief that the probability of success is significantly increased when an "opportunity meets preparation." The mental preparation required to succeed continues far beyond the first day on the job. Measured and gradual adjustments to strengthen and sharpen mental focus must occur as the realities and details of a particular leadership challenge unfold.

The initial steps of the *Focused Leadership* approach encompass the process of preparing yourself intellectually as well as psychologically for the situation at hand. Prior to fully embracing a new leadership role, I remind myself of a quote attributed to William Shakespeare, *"All things are ready, if our minds are ready."* The two questions I consistently ask myself in order to prepare to focus on a leadership challenge are "How should I lead this particular effort to achieve the desired results" and "What will my world and my team's world look like at the end of this journey?"

From leading scores of teams and projects over the past thirty years and having experimented with various leadership styles, I have come to believe that *leading with intention*, versus depending on your authority, gets far better results. Correspondingly, establishing a clear vision of where you are taking your team and creating an effective method to communicate that vision both "upward" and "downward" are imperatives.

In this chapter, I elaborate on these observations and reveal the first two steps of the *Focused Leadership* approach to leading and winning. However, first, here's an anecdote that will help set the stage for understanding the concepts involved.

ANECDOTE

FIRST CLASSIFIED DOD SPACE SHUTTLE MISSION

AT 4:23 P.M. EST on January 27, 1985 the Space Shuttle Discovery appeared to touch down without a hitch at the Kennedy Space Center in Florida after successfully completing its mission and traveling a total of 1.3 million miles.

None of the tens of thousands observing the magnificent landing of this space ship were aware that during the planned external tank separation, the backup flight system (BFS) did not automatically proceed to the proper landing mode. The crew of five astronauts, including the Commander, Thomas

Mattingly and Pilot Loren Shriver, had to quickly react and perform the necessary manual procedures to resume normal landing operations. The BFS operated satisfactorily until the Shuttle's final deorbit maneuver. For some reason, the BFS deorbit maneuver ignition was 8 seconds late. Fortunately, the BFS miraculously operated satisfactorily from that point for a safe touch down and landing.

There were many other significant behind the scene maneuvers that contributed to the successful mission of what was called STS-51-C. However, without one much larger behind the scene maneuver that started several years earlier, STS-51-C's mission would not have been possible.

This mission critical maneuver involved a well-coordinated and massive effort to retrofit the Space Shuttle with a special capability required in order for STS-51-C to accomplish its sensitive mission. This complicated project would eventually consist of hundreds of trained professionals, millions of contract-related dollars, a magnificent technology deployment and a remarkable leadership feat.

STS-51-C was the first classified Department of Defense (DoD) mission of the Space Shuttle. The U.S. National Aeronautic and Space Administration (NASA) Space Transportation System (STS) vehicle was rolled out in 1981. The STS, more commonly known as the Space Shuttle, was the first operational orbital spacecraft designed for reuse.

It carried different payloads into low earth orbit. It provided crew rotation for the International Space Station (ISS). It also performed servicing missions. The orbiter could recover satellites and other payloads from orbit and return them to Earth. Each Shuttle was designed for a projected lifespan of 100 launches or ten years of operational life, although this was later extended. The crucial factor in the size and shape of the Shuttle Orbiter was the requirement that it be able to accommodate the largest planned commercial and military satellites. The Shuttle's cross-range recovery capability also met all of the requirements for classified USAF missions.

However, the original design of the Shuttle's sophisticated communications system did not include a strategic security capability required to support all DoD missions. This capability would provide a classified level of encryption for all voice, data and telemetry communications.

The development of the complex ground-based and space-borne equipment required to accomplish the retrofit of the Space Shuttle with this capability was started in the late 1970's and code named Project Elwell.

The Elwell development and initial production contract was competitively awarded to the

Government Electronics Division of Motorola, Inc. The technical challenge involved the design & development of the ground-based and space-borne encryption equipment as well as the monumental task of coordinating the effort with the associated tri-service (Army, Navy and Air Force) projects. The Elwell project team would also have to design the equipment such that it could be physically and electronically retrofitted into a "fixed-footprint" or form factor which was dictated by the original design of the Space Shuttle vehicle.

A couple of years prior to the planned launch of STS-51-C, the difficult development effort was successfully completed and tested. By 1982, the focus had shifted to the critical delivery of the production grade equipment required to retrofit the Space Shuttle fleet and ensure that the first planned DoD mission could be accomplished on schedule.

The Elwell production contract was also awarded to Motorola's Government Electronics Division. Motorola would organize the project into a matrix-managed program team to accomplish the contract's objectives. That is, a team comprised of hundreds of engineering, manufacturing, materials procurement, quality management and production professionals reporting to a single Elwell Production Program Manager, but only on a dotted-line basis. The production team members would get their direction from the Program Manager for the execution of the Elwell Production contract but still report to their respective functional departments for performance and salary reviews.

This Elwell production team would eventually manufacture and deliver a large number of highly reliable ground-based and space-borne units on multiple contracts exceeding $100 million over several years. This would include, of course, the successful delivery of the equipment required to enable the January 24, 1985 launch of Space Shuttle Discovery and the STS-51-C mission.

The Elwell Production Program team also succeeded in establishing itself as a high performance team within Motorola. The team exceeded all internal quality goals despite difficult material procurement challenges. The Elwell Production team was one of the first production teams to be awarded over a million dollars in special performance bonuses based on exceeding pre-determined quality and cost reduction targets.

I feel privileged to have had the opportunity to serve as the Elwell Production Program Manager and to lead the Elwell Production team during this momentous period. As a relatively new program manager, this was my first major experience in leading a multifaceted mix of professional talent in a true matrix management environment. At its peak, my expanded Elwell Production team numbered over 300 team members.

We were able to maintain an intense focus on executing a complex project under intense schedule pressure and design constraints. I quickly learned that leading this type of team, without the authority of a "solid line" reporting relationship, required me to prepare myself for every turn along the way. After some initial "ego bruising" and unexpected disappointments, I realized that in order to be successful in this particular leadership role, I would have to build the team's trust in my ability to articulate the "big picture" as well as the details surrounding the technical and production challenges. I would also have to confidently lead with enduring intention.

With a peer leadership team spanning much of NASA, DoD (including the Army, Air Force and Navy) and the National Security Agency, keeping a flawless focus on the project's purpose was a must. Just as important was the need for me to envision, from the start, how the project would end and keep a laser focus on the path to success.

I made it a point during every morning "stand-up" meeting with the Elwell Production team to clearly update everyone on our purpose, our goals, our status and our daily & monthly objectives. At 30 years of age, I found myself regularly engaging with talented engineers and skilled production assembly team members as well as three-star military Generals. I was fully cognizant of and respected the fact that I was viewed, at all levels, as the final decision-maker regarding critical performance requirements and delivery commitments. I realized that I was not just the Production Program Manager. I was the designated leader of a passionate, cross-functional team that was depending on me and my leadership to ensure the project's success.

When the Space Shuttle Discovery touched down at 4:23 p.m. EST on January 27, 1985, it also brought home 385 special Elwell badges that traveled the complete 1.3 million miles of the mission. A few months after the successful STS-51-C mission, I was proud to be a part of a recognition ceremony where each of the Elwell Production team members were given one of these special badges.

To this day, I place extraordinary value on the badge I received that day and on the lessons in leadership I learned during that stage of my management career.

"The will to win is worthless if you do not have the will to prepare."

---Thane Yost

LEAD WITH INTENTION, NOT AUTHORITY.

I MUST ADMIT that when I was promoted to my first leadership position I was not aware that there were so many documented leadership styles. From Autocratic to Democratic to Laissez-faire and from Mahatma Gandhi to Winston Churchill to Martin Luther King, there are as many leadership styles as there are leaders. Most experts in the field of leadership would agree that to become a more effective leader, it is important to develop your own, personal leadership style.

Common to all styles of leadership is the availability and the use of authority. Of course, some level of authority is essential in order to achieve leadership success within any organizational context. This is especially the case when it comes to managing situations across and up the organizational structure. However, my personal experience overwhelmingly suggests that to more effectively lead those in the organization below you to the best possible outcome, gaining the respect and commitment through clarity of direction and mutual expectations is essential. Leading with intention means that your ultimate goal as a leader is to add value to your organization, gain the commitment of others and develop & deploy all of the talents of your team members --- all while sustaining loyalty. Thus, the *Focused Leadership* approach emphasizes the concept of leading with intention.

Step-1
LEADING WITH INTENTION, NOT AUTHORITY

WHAT TO DO TODAY	WHAT YOU WILL GAIN	WHAT YOU WILL AVOID
Express clearly your wants, needs and desires.	Being perceived as a visionary who knows what is needed to achieve the team's goals.	Organizational confusion regarding what is needed and what you desire.
Go out of your way to show respect for other's points of view.	The trust and mutual respect of your team.	The perception that only your point of view matters.
Listen with intent to understand what is really being said.	Valuable insight into what your team is really thinking.	Being "blind-sided" by what your team thinks of you.
Take the time to appraise your team's talents and developmental needs.	The vision you need to effectively deploy and develop your team.	Not having the talent and skills required to accomplish your goals.
Appraise any skills deficiencies you may have which might impact your success on this particular challenge.	The insight needed to devise a timely plan to "plug-the-holes" and increase the probability of success.	Not being prepared for the task at hand. Having only "four-cylinders" when "six cylinders" are needed.

FOCUSED

"Imagination is not only the uniquely human capacity to envision that which is not, and therefore the fount of all invention and innovation. In its arguably most transformative and revelatory capacity, it is the power that enables us to empathize with humans whose experiences we have never shared."

---J.K.Rowling

FOCUSED LEADERSHIP

WHEN MY FIRST corporate mentor told me that in order to lead a team to the results that you expect, you must yourself be able to see "the big picture," I thought I understood what he meant. It wasn't until I failed to accomplish my first major goal and had the time to reflect on what went wrong, did I began to realize the true complexities associated with visualizing and articulating "the big picture."

The big picture of a scenario is the broader perspective or objective, not the fine detail. The big picture includes a fundamental understanding of what is needed in order to successfully arrive at the destination. In addition, it must include a "roadmap" indicating how to get from here to there. As I matured as a leader, I gained and began to value my ability to envision and share with my team a broader perspective of our mission. That is, not just how we would reach our goals but also "why" we, as a team, were doing it.

As I mentioned in this chapter's anecdote, *"The Elwell Production Program team also succeeded in establishing itself as a high performance team within Motorola."* I knew from day one of the Elwell Production Program that in order for this team to be successful in ensuring the launch of the STS-51-C mission, we would also have to achieve "sub-goals" along the way. One of them was to become one of Motorola's most highly regarded production teams.

Step-2
ENVISION THE END AT THE START

WHAT TO DO TODAY	WHAT YOU WILL GAIN	WHAT YOU WILL AVOID
Write a personal essay which articulately defines all the aspects of your vision and what the "Big Picture" entails.	A crisp, coherent understanding of your vision. The visibility to clearly identify any short-falls or "disconnects" prior to sharing.	Change or corrections to the vision and/or the "Big Picture" later. Unintended and possible distracting variations normally associated with "undocumented" visions.
Do whatever you must to ensure that others "see your vision."	A widely known, clearly understood and shared vision.	Portions of your vision not understood by your team members.
Paint the "Big Picture" vividly and make sure it includes all vital "sub-goals" and "sub-challenges."	Complete "buy-in" to all components and phases of the challenge. Team commitment even when "heavy lifting" is required.	Any "fuzziness" or ambiguity regarding what to expect and what has to be done to be successful.
Keep your eyes on the horizon and not just on the activity at hand.	The "view" you will need to "steer the ship" and keep things on course.	Missing the target or getting "side-tracked."

"The truth is that teamwork is at the heart of great achievement."

John Maxwell

CHAPTER TWO

PREPARING YOUR TEAM TO WIN

"You were born to win, but to be a winner, you must plan to win, prepare to win, and expect to win."

Zig Ziglar

PREPARING YOUR TEAM TO WIN

THE ABILITY TO PREPARE your team to win is a critical factor regardless of the type of organization you are leading. People must work closely together, sometimes wear multiple hats and work effectively across the organization. As Zig Ziglar once said "winning is not everything, but the effort to win is."

In order for me, as a leader, to successfully encourage the proper level of collaboration and interdependency that high performance teams must have, I had to learn over the years how to support and prepare my teams to win, both mentally and psychologically.

Early in my career, I was asked to attend a course on business psychology. Not surprisingly, the course focused primarily on strategically maximizing an organization's most important assets --- its people.

To achieve maximum performance, it recommended that, as a manger and leader, you must be sensitive to and recognize the impact that organizational behavior has on the bottom line of any organization. It also stressed the importance of creating a synergistic balance between training, communications and teamwork. Over the years, while leading large and small teams, I have found success in keeping these three areas in focus while preparing my teams to win.

A winning team must have the resources and training required to develop the skills needed to effectively do its job. Since not every person is capable of doing every job, preparation starts with ensuing that team members are properly matched with the job that best fits his or her skills and ability. If you were not involved in the initial selection of the team, then your focus should be to quickly assess each team member and make strategic adjustments as opportunities for personnel changes surface.

Team communication is a crucial feature for a team to function effectively and dynamically. However, team communication differs from normal communications with respect to the difficulty of conveying the same message across the organization. Fostering "high performance" teams requires creating a work culture that values collaboration. All of your team members must understand and believe that thinking, planning, arriving at decisions and taking actions are better when done cooperatively.

I cannot over stress the importance of team coordination, especially in critical phases of a project or task. A perfect example is presented in this chapter's anecdote. You should note the following excerpt --- *"All the tremendous resources available to the U.S. military ---from spy satellites to the Marines --- had been marshaled for the purpose of rescuing O'Grady, and they had been deployed with flawless coordination."*

Based on my experience, the best way to prepare a team to win and to be psychologically ready to function as a team is to build a shared vision. Since a team's preparation is a continuous process, as a leader, you must articulate your vision, repeatedly.

I believe the following anecdote, *Rescuing Scott O'Grady,* builds a convincing case for how important it is for a team to be mentally and psychologically prepared to win.

"Leaders must invoke an alchemy of great vision."

Henry A. Kissinger

ANECDOTE

RESCUING SCOTT O'GRADY

SO PERFECTLY was the mission executed that it amazed even the men responsible. At 2:08 a.m. Central European time, on June 8, 1995 Air Force Captain Scott O'Grady was sitting, as he had for six days, cold, hungry, hunted and alone in the hills of a strange country.

Then he made contact with a U.S. plane. By 7:30 a.m. he was onboard the U.S.S. Kearsarge, a once missing soldier now safely back among his comrades. All the tremendous resources available to the U.S. military --- from spy satellites to the Marines --- had been marshaled for the purpose of rescuing O'Grady, and they had been deployed with flawless coordination.

It had begun six days before, when his F-16 was targeted by an SA-6 surface-to-air missile fired from a Bosnian-Serb stronghold just south of Bihac. But miraculously, O'Grady had managed to safely eject. As he landed in a grassy clearing, O'Grady wasted no time. In seconds, he had shed his parachute and was dashing toward a small clump of bushes.

The downed flyer had soon consumed the eight 4-oz. packs of water in his emergency kit. But he was able to catch rain in Ziploc plastic bags and at one point tried to squeeze water out of his wet woolen socks, without much luck. He found nourishment by eating leaves, grass and ants --- but not too many of the latter.

The 29-lb. survival kit strapped under the seat of O'Grady's F-16 contained a first-aid kit, a few flares, some radio batteries and a 9-mm pistol, among other items. In his vest, O'Grady also had an "evasion chart" --- a waterproof map with pointers on how to survive in northwestern Bosnia. The map included cues for edible plants such as dandelion, licorice root and nettle. His most important asset was a 28-oz. PRC-112. The PRC-112 is a survival radio, barely larger than a Walkman. The highly reliable radio is designed to operate for as long as seven hours on a single battery. Its ability to broadcast a locating beep, Morse code or voice is perfect for search and rescue missions.

O'Grady's efforts to establish contact using the PRC were thwarted at first by bad weather, which kept allied planes away for several days. Undaunted, he kept on the move, searching as best he could in the dark for a locale with three critical attributes: a clear high point to broadcast from, a place suitable for a large helicopter to land, but one not too vulnerable to enemy fire.

Not until Tuesday evening, nearly five days after the shoot-down, did NATO planes flying over the region finally confirm that they were getting more extensive transmissions from what was thought to be O'Grady's radio beacon.

The PRC-112 survival radio was one of the military assets that played a key role in the rescue of Captain Scott O'Grady on June 8, 1995. The PRC-112 radio used by O'Grady was one of thousands of PRC-112 radios manufactured by Motorola, Inc. under a U.S. Government contract.

I was the Vice President of Motorola's Radio Systems Operations at the time. I was responsible for Motorola's worldwide military and civil radio products business.

My responsibilities also included leading the PRC-112 engineering and production teams. Our goal was to ensure that every PRC-112 radio met the highest levels of quality standards. From the initial design of the PRC-112 to the deployment of the six-sigma-based production processes, our vision was to deliver the most reliable radio of its type available to our elite military forces.

During the production years of the PRC-112 Program, all of the support team members were carefully chosen and they all understood the magnitude of the task at hand. As a team, we were all committed to our goal to ensure that from the first radio produced --- to the last --- every PRC-112 must be ready for any mission around the world.

As the executive member of the leadership team, I was routinely involved in addressing all design and production challenges. I fondly recall spending countless hours with our engineering team members as well as the two-star General who was ultimately responsible for the Air Force PRC-112 procurement. My focus was to proactively resolve, in real time, all concerns which may have eroded the military's confidence in the reliability of the radio.

I am proud to say that as a focused team, we successfully accomplished our goals. As a result, my PRC-112 team played a major role in the successful rescue of Scott O'Grady.

Articulate your vision, repeatedly.

IF YOU ARE at the very top of your company, leading a team or unit of a large organization or leading a small group of individuals toward a destination, they all think you know where you are going.

Articulating your vision is an instrumental part of being a leader. Having a vision in your head and your heart is just simply not enough. Many people have visions that they keep to themselves. But, as a leader, your vision for your organization and how your team will achieve its goal must be shared.

Research has shown that a well-crafted and skillfully articulated vision can even draw more commitment from a team than just charisma alone. But, it's only when you take the time to share your vision with your team that you will find the support and commitment that cannot be found otherwise.

A skillfully articulated vision enables your team to be aligned with you. The leadership vision goes beyond a written statement. It permeates the workplace and becomes manifested in the actions, beliefs, values and goals of your organization. However, you must continually enforce and reinforce your team's movement toward the vision. This is why Step-3 of the *Focus Leadership* approach to leading and winning emphasizes the need for you to articulate your vision, repeatedly.

Step-3
ARTICULATE YOUR VISION, REPEATEDLY

WHAT TO DO TODAY	WHAT YOU WILL GAIN	WHAT YOU WILL AVOID
Keep it simple. What is the future you intend to create? What do you see in that vision? What do you need from your team? How will you and the team feel when you all arrive at your destination?	A crisp, coherent and shared understanding of your vision by your team members.	Team members being confused and possibly disillusioned by a long presentation that is soon forgotten.
Paint a Picture	Your team's attention and their ability to retain a vision which paints a picture versus just words.	Not clearly getting your vision and message across to the team.
Keep the sharing a regular event	Team commitment and loyalty --- Being constantly reminded that what you are fighting and working for has intrinsic value.	Forgetfulness --- People need to be reminded of the reason they're doing things. It's only natural to forget after a while.

"Good business leaders create a vision, articulate the vision, passionately own the vision and relentlessly drive it to completion."

---Jack Welch

CHAPTER THREE

SETTING TACTICAL PARAMETERS

"Strategy requires thought, tactics require observation."

---Max Euve

SETTING TACTICAL PARAMETERS

HAVING SPENT MORE than a decade leading technology programs and production efforts for a major U.S. Defense contractor, I have been exposed to many of the tactical and strategic approaches that the U.S. Military has devised over the years to foster a culture of winning.

Of course, from a military perspective, particular words have particular meanings. In the military, "winning" is thought of in terms of fully accomplishing the mission with minimum or no loss of life. From the perspective of a civilian organization, winning also centers around successfully accomplishing a mission. However, the major secondary objectives are usually of a different flavor --- such as "at a minimum expense" or "for maximum customer, stakeholder and employee satisfaction."

In the military, the words tactical intelligence also has a special meaning. It refers to the art or science of determining what the opposition is doing, or might do, to prevent the accomplishment of your mission. Ironically, over the years my perspective of tactical leadership within civilian settings has also shifted in this direction.

Experiences that I have had in the most recent phase of my professional career have led me to this conclusion. It seems that at times, the most effective approach to "tactical" leadership is to not only focus on "what you <u>are</u> doing" but to also focus some attention on "what you <u>are</u> <u>not</u> doing." Ironically, this opposing view will allow you to more easily recognize what might be lurking and might disrupt the accomplishment of your mission.

The reasoning here is somewhat analogous to the military's definition of tactical intelligence. Just as in the military, unforeseen tactical challenges or hurdles can willingly or unknowingly work against your team's efforts to "win the war." To prevent major distractions, these so called "known-unknowns" must be recognized in a timely fashion. In addition, as the leader, you must define and make your team aware of the "parameters" (or guidelines) that they should follow as they respond to such hurdles.

Your team members should be more than capable of addressing what's in front of them today. However, it is the role of leadership to set the team's course such that they are in the best position to adequately *respond* and not just *react* to the tactical "mayhem" which might be around the corner tomorrow or next week.

In this chapter you will find a candid and somewhat unusual anecdote titled, *"Leading Change During Times of Unchartered Circumstance."* The anecdote attempts to summarize in a few short pages a *year-long gallop* that I took through the world of "venture capital-backed," start-up companies.

As you will note when you read this anecdote, much of the story's script is used to paint a rather tactical picture of the landscape I found myself in as I was challenged to lead an organization which was encountering change on many critical fronts. I unfortunately experienced the anguish and futility of leading an organization that was not prepared to counter the devastating impact that can be associated with a colossal dose of tactical "mayhem."

However, the lesson that I learned from having the courage to step into this once-in-a-lifetime opportunity was a true character builder. I will allow you to appreciate the significance of this lesson in the context as presented in the anecdote. All I will say here is that leadership, as with most things in life, has its limitations.

In addition, you will also be introduced in this chapter to three more steps of the *Focused Leadership* approach to becoming a more effective leader. The discussions in all three steps include modest but powerful actions you can implement today. Once implemented, they will help you frame your team's focus and help steer them beyond "hurdles" which might threaten your organization's success.

"One reason so few of us achieve what we truly want is that we never direct our focus."

---Anthony Robbins

ANECDOTE

LEADING CHANGE DURING TIMES OF UNCHARTERED CIRCUMSTANCE

MedContrax Names Earl Cobb Chief Operating Officer

Business Editors/Health & Medical Writers BIOWIRE2K

GAITHERSBURG, Md.--(BW HealthWire)--May 9, 2001--MedContrax(TM) Inc., the leading healthcare contracting information and network solution provider, today announced the appointment of Ervin (Earl) Cobb as chief operating officer. As COO, Cobb will direct day-to-day operations and be responsible for P&L for the company's entire contracting and sales information solutions business and will report directly to Randy Hoggle, CEO and President of MedContrax.

"Earl is an excellent and timely addition to our senior management team as we continue to commercialize our Contract Processing Network (CPN) and establish a world-class business operation," said Randy Hoggle. "His broad technical background, Fortune 50 management experience and proven organizational leadership abilities will assist MedContrax in its efforts to improve the operating efficiencies of its customers."

MedContrax Signs Manufacturer Agreement with Procter & Gamble Pharmaceuticals

Editor - Apr 3, 2001

The MedContrax CPN will act as a neutral third-party interface between Procter & Gamble Pharmaceuticals, pharmaceutical distributors and group purchasing organizations (GPOs). The agreement will enable Procter & Gamble, distributors and GPO's to participate in the MedContrax network to utilize Web-based technologies and securely create and document valid contract pricing for the end users, via non-repudiable purchasing agreements online.

Novation to Use MedContrax's CPN for Pharmacy Contracting Process
May 23, 2001

MedContrax Inc., the leading healthcare contracting infrastructure company, today announced that Novation, the supply company of VHA Inc. and the University HealthSystem Consortium, has agreed to use MedContrax's Contract Processing Network (CPN™) to facilitate development of Novation's new $6 billion pharmacy portfolio later this year. Novation is the largest supply cost management company in healthcare, managing more than $15 billion in annual purchases on behalf of more than 7,000 healthcare organizations nationwide.

Premier, Inc. Selects MedContrax's CPN for Pharmacy Contracting Process; MedContrax, the Only Independent Contracting Solution.

Business Editors/Health & Medical Writers
BIOWIRE2K

GAITHERSBURG, Md.--(BW HealthWire)--July 2, 2001

MedContrax Inc., the leading healthcare contract network solution company, today announced that Premier, Inc., one of the nation's leading healthcare alliances, has chosen to use MedContrax's Contract Processing Network (CPN(TM)) to manage their multi-billion dollar pharmacy portfolio and create greater contracting cost efficiencies. Premier will utilize the MedContrax CPN to facilitate the maintenance and administration of its pharmaceutical contracts.

Bloomberg Businessweek

As of July 9, 2002, MedContrax, Inc. was acquired by Neoforma Inc. MedContrax, Inc., formerly known, as SynTegra HealthCare Management Services, Inc., is a healthcare contracting network application solution provider (NASP) that offers a programming web based solution to the healthcare contracting process. The MedContrax network service provides pharmaceutical trading partners with control of contracting documents through a third-party interface.

With sale of division, MedContrax ceases to be

Washington Business Journal - by Chris Silva, Staff Reporter
Date: Friday, August 2, 2002, 2:38pm EDT

MedContrax, a Gaithersburg health care services provider, has finalized the sale of its subsidiary, Med-ecorp, to Neoforma, a health care solutions company based in San Jose, Calif. With the sale of Med-ecorp complete, operations of MedContrax effectively have ceased. The company, which provided contract processing and data integration services to the health care industry, filed for Chapter 11 bankruptcy earlier this year, says Jordi Guso, an attorney with Berger Singerman. Guso says MedContrax was a victim of tough market conditions. MedContrax "exhausted all working capital and didn't have the ability to recruit new sources of capital," Guso says. MedContrax's investors included Salix Ventures, Pacific Venture Group, Cardinal Partners and Oxford Bioscience Partners.

AT APPROXIMATELY 11:00 a.m. EST on September 11, 2001, I found myself leaving Dupont Circle on the Washington Metro Red Line heading to the Shady Grove Metro Station and back to my office in Gaithersburg, Maryland. As I looked around a packed train, almost everyone on board had a government ID badge attached to a lanyard hanging around their necks. They all were like me --- still in shock and wondering what had just happened to our country. Once separated by two great oceans and immune from the actual horror of war, every American's life had changed and would never be the same.

In addition to the concern of what impact the 9/11 terror attacks would have on life in America over the coming days and months, my thoughts at that moment also centered around the potential impact the unthinkable event might have on MedContrax, Inc. --- the young technology start-up company that I was leading at the time. Most of my concern was regarding the MedContrax team. They had worked so hard over the past twelve months to turn a vision into a viable commercial reality.

As I walked into my Gaithersburg office around 12:30 p.m., most of my staff members and a dozen or so employees were in the main lobby. My Chief Financial Officer was also in the lobby. He shared with me that those employees who wanted to go home for the afternoon were permitted to do so. We all gathered around the television for the rest of the afternoon watching the latest news regarding the horrifying terrorist attacks.

I was in my office later than usual on the evening of September 11th. I was on the phone most of the night with members of the MedContrax Board of Directors. I had just returned from New York City the night before. My CFO and I had spent most of that day making a pitch to the investment bank of Bear Stearns. We were hoping to get them to join the team of MedContrax investors. We had been working feverously for months to finalize a second round of venture funding.

While coming home on the train from New York that evening, I felt that the day's presentations had gone well. I knew that if Bear Stearns agreed to join the second round of financing, we would be able to close a deal. I got up early on the morning of September 11th. I took the Metro into Washington that morning to make a presentation to a group of Angel investors. This was not the first pitch I had made to this group. We were counting on them to also buy into the second round of financing. This level of venture investor would always wait until major investors had taken the lead. I was standing in front of the group that morning when the cell phones began to ring. The news was unfolding regarding the plane which had just slammed into the Pentagon a few miles down the street.

As the newly appointed President and CEO of MedContrax, I could only be optimistic. But, deep inside, I hoped that the circumstances surrounding the attacks would not delay a favorable decision by our potential second round investors. MedContrax had only a few months of cash remaining in the bank. I knew that obtaining another major bridge loan from our current investment partners would now be even more difficult. Furthermore, my experience and my gut told me that it would be a very difficult chore for me, or anyone, to change the course of the unchartered circumstances that the 9/11 attacks were about to set in motion throughout the financial world.

By sequentially reading the news headlines and associated briefings at the beginning of this anecdote, you most likely have already gained sufficient insight into how this story unfolds and the eventual fate of MedContrax, Inc. Two of the questions that may have come to mind and remain unanswered at this point might be:

1) How did I move so quickly from the role of COO to become the Company's President and CEO; and

2) Why was the task to keep MedContrax afloat after the 9/11 attacks not successful?

Well, here is the rest of the story and the lesson I learned about leading change during times of unchartered circumstance. The best place to start is from the beginning.

I first became aware of the leadership challenges surrounding MedContrax, Inc. during a meeting in Chicago's O'Hare airport in January 2001. One of the company's board members, who also represented one of the three main private equity investors, had scheduled the meeting to discuss the possibility of me accepting the role as MedContrax's first Chief Operating Officer. Matt was smart, savvy and definitely in control. I was quite impressed with his demeanor and the respect he appeared to have for my background and experience.

I had recently completed a stint as Vice President of Operations for the Reynolds & Reynolds Healthcare Systems Division in Dayton, Ohio --- a stint that was cut short by the sale of the Healthcare Systems Division and Reynolds & Reynolds' exit from the healthcare systems business in 1999. The move from Motorola, Inc. to Reynolds & Reynolds in 1997 represented a change from a leadership role in a Fortune 50 to one in a Fortune 500 size company. Even with annual sales revenues of around a billion dollars, I quickly recognized the more entrepreneurial nature of my role within Reynolds & Reynolds as compared to most of my 18 years with Motorola. I was very much aware that a move to a venture start-up company, like MedContrax, would require another magnitude of leadership adjustment and present a different entrepreneurial challenge. Of course, firmly sketched in the back of my mind (from years of management lessons learned) was the realization that the primary difference between leading your own [or what seems like your own] business versus someone else's can be summarized in a four letter word --- RISK.

Needless to say, as announced in the first news headline included in the beginning of this anecdote, I accepted the position and moved into a new leadership role as the first COO of MedContrax in February 2001. On the other hand, what the hiring announcement does not indicate is the fact that the incumbent management team had already burned through the entire first round of venture funding.

Since its inception in 1998, MedContrax was viewed internally and portrayed as a technology company. During the opportunity hungry times of dot-com era investing, it might have been the correct image for a company requiring start-up financing to portray. However, under the leadership of the incumbent team, the company also spent heavily on technology, technologists and technical processes.

It was true that the transaction management technology and the ability to automate the rather complex pharmaceutical contracting processes were fundamental to MedContrax's business model. However, for MedContrax to quickly gain market presence and attract paying customers, it had to first be perceived as an independent, viable and trustworthy transactional services company.

As a result of historical management decisions, MedContrax was entering the critical product commercialization and market penetration phase with only "bridge funding" being periodically provided by the three main venture investors. I knew that by accepting the role of MedContrax COO, I was also accepting the fact that, due to the funding situation, the incumbent team must be transformed into my "turn-around" team.

From the first day in my new role, it became apparent that there was no time to waste. While the CEO continued his bid to attract new investors and new money, I was busy figuring out how to reduce the cost of the initial rollout of MedContrax's flagship technology platform called the Contract Processing Network (CPN). At the same time, I had to quickly build a marketing/sales team and pen as many agreements with new pharmaceutical trading partners as possible.

The press releases at the beginning of this anecdote reflect the initial success we were having in attracting some rather large and well-respected pharmaceutical trading partners into the fold of MedContrax. The likes of companies and Group Purchasing Organizations such as Proctor & Gamble, Novation and Premier significantly enhanced our chances of establishing business traction. Such traction was critical to our efforts to convince new venture partners that an investment in a second round of MedContrax funding would be a wise move.

Now, that you have a deeper sense of the tactical nature and diversity of the MedContrax challenges, I will now bring this story to its rightful conclusion. I will first address the two questions we touched on earlier. Then, I will share with you the lesson I learned regarding leadership and the challenge associated with leading change during times of unchartered circumstance.

1) How did I move so quickly from the role of COO to become the Company's President and CEO?

As the months rolled by without a deal on the second round of funding, the MedContrax Board of Directors became more and more impatient with the incumbent CEO. In an attempt to "shake things up" the Board thought that I had a better chance of securing a second round of funding and elevated me to the President and CEO post. They asked the incumbent CEO to accept a VP of Marketing role and lead the company's critical marketing & sales effort. To make a long story short, after some classical drama, he resigned from the company instead. Thus, after less than a year with the company and, as fate would have it, I found myself responsible for leading the entire organization.

2) *Why was the task to keep MedContrax afloat after the 9/11 attacks not successful?*

After the 9/11 attacks, the definition of "keeping MedContrax afloat" changed significantly.

Prior to 9/11 my leadership challenge was to create enough business traction to keep both the current investment partners and potential investors believing that the dollars they invest in MedContrax would continue to offer as much potential "upside" as any alternative investment opportunity.

With 9/11 came a major collapse of the U.S. financial markets and the burst of the "dot-com" bubble. Thus, after the 9/11 attacks, the definition of "keeping MedContrax afloat" was transformed into stretching the last few dollars of the bridge funding that remained and executing a survival strategy. The burst of the dot-com bubble was an unchartered circumstance. It inevitably created a situation where a record number of young start-up hi tech companies had to spontaneously compete for a rapidly shrinking pool of venture capital. For those companies which had not already gained operational traction and growing revenue streams, like MedContrax, finding new investment dollars was near impossible.

The lesson I learned from the MedContrax experience about leading change during times of unchartered circumstance was two-fold.

The first part of the lesson can be summarized as follows --- *when facing a situation involving highly unusual and unchartered circumstances, the true challenge associated with leading change is getting beyond the present and envisioning a future beyond the circumstance.* I quickly realized that without any "dry powder" (the private equity vernacular for cash in the bank), a merger or liquidation were the only viable options. A merger could possibly create a chance for the MedContrax employees and the Contract Processing Network to have a future. As a last resort, liquidation, under bankruptcy protection, would protect the current investors from additional liabilities.

Within a week after 9/11, the Board of Directors and I hired a small San Francisco based investment banker to find a merger partner for MedContrax. The effort revealed that an asset auction was the most probable course of action within the existing time constraints. When the auction was announced, several interested companies quickly surfaced. However, once they completed their due diligence of the MedContrax assets, they all decided to just wait until we ran out of cash and take their chances on being able to acquire the MedContrax assets at a lower cost during bankruptcy.

In the end, MedContrax's fate was shaped on 9/11 and sealed by the company's inability to re-position itself following the fall of the dot-com era.

The second part of the lesson is that, at times, it is important to remember that *"it's not all about you."*

As leaders, we generally have a mindset that there is no challenge too large or too difficult. It's simply a matter of the right strategy, enough time and adequate resources. In what can be considered "normal" circumstances, the most challenging results can sometimes be achieved by more personal and active leadership involvement. However, many times when unchartered circumstances are involved, achieving the desired results may require sluggish change to entrenched systems, institutions or markets that rarely retort to any one individual or a single event.

As a leader, you must be passionate and stay focused under all circumstances. You must do all that you can to touch everyone and everything required to succeed. However, to preserve what makes you an effective leader --- your attitude and your strong sense of self --- you must also be realistic about changing things that certain circumstances remove entirely from your control.

"Leadership and learning are indispensable to each other."

---John F. Kennedy

Don't allow bumps in the road to distract you.

ALTHOUGH I SPENT only five years directly practicing my craft as an electrical engineer, it is my engineering training that laid the foundation from which I see and manage my world. However, coming in at a close second are the tactical planning and project execution skills I developed during ten years of program and project management assignments.

One rule that I would establish with my program teams at the onset of each new challenge would always be "let's not allow bumps in the road to distract us." In the tactical world of leadership, it's all about knowing where the trees are, but not getting lost in the forest. A good project or business plan will include all of the activities required to successfully achieve its objectives. The plan will also take into account all of the known "bumps" that may be encountered along the road to success.

But, experience has taught me that it's the "known-unknowns" which surface at the worst time that create the most distraction and add the most risk to completing all aspects of the project on schedule and within budget. From my perspective, "known-unknowns" are things that are predictable but not predicted and not accounted for in your current financial or human resource plans.

I have found that the best way to be prepared to minimize the distraction and potential impact that may be caused by tactical surprises is to maximize communications at all levels of your organization. The sooner you, as the leader, are aware that something unsuspecting is lurking, the sooner you can assess the potential impact and adjust all activities that might be affected accordingly.

I recall being told by a mentor and seasoned program manager that "the most welcomed partner of anything which has a mission of causing havoc to a set of the best laid plans is the lack of open, honest and timely communications among all who are involved."

Step-4 of the *Focused Leadership* approach to becoming a more effective leader emphasizes the need to create a workplace environment which clings to a robust culture of open, honest and timely communications.

Step-4
DON'T ALLOW BUMPS IN THE ROAD TO DISTRACT YOU

WHAT TO DO TODAY	WHAT YOU WILL GAIN	WHAT YOU WILL AVOID
Establish an "open door" policy. It should allow any team member to schedule a meeting with you.	The perception of your team that you are accessible and want to be informed.	The failure of your team to share important and timely information about the project or business.
Hold regular "cross-functional" team meetings.	The opportunity for all functional areas to openly communicate.	Potential tactical hurdles being masked by functional lines.
Conduct informal "scenario planning" sessions with your direct reports.	A common mind-set regarding how the team would handle certain predictable but not accounted for situations.	Scrambling during the "heat of the battle" to devise and communicate a plan of action.
Incorporate the idea of establishing reserves (schedule and budget) as a part of your normal planning cycle.	Some degree of built-in margin to address "known-unknowns." A culture of "putting some away for a rainy day."	Being caught with no "margin for mayhem" and having to absorb the full schedule and/or financial impact.

Energize others to do their best.

AS THE LEADER, you have a powerful effect on your team. When you walk into a room, your team members feel either taller or smaller. Yet, many unfocused leaders are often not conscious of this important aspect and responsibility of leadership.

As a leader, you have more power than you think. Conversely, you will also get more out of what you focus on. When you focus on energizing and empowering your entire team, you will not only make your team members feel taller when you walk in the room, you will also reap the rewards of improved performance and increased commitment to the task at hand.

In my experience, you can easily energize your team members by maintaining a positive view of their contribution and proactively sharing this perception with them. This includes letting them know that you think they are smart and hardworking, expressing gratitude for their efforts, reminding them why their work is important to the mission and emphasizing the difference they are making to the organization.

Conversely, empowerment requires more focus, attention and involvement. First of all, empowerment is more than delegation. It is also more than just sharing your power and your authority with others. Empowerment involves determining the level of power and authority you are willing to give and the level that your team members are willing to accept.

However, the independent entrepreneurship and initiative gained through empowerment will lead to higher levels of team member energy, contribution, commitment, engagement, innovation, productivity and involvement in decision making.

Within the framework of the *Focused Leadership* approach, proactively energizing and empowering your team is a powerful catalyst for maximizing team member contributions and achieving maximum performance. Then, you must provide the coaching and tactical direction required to obtain the desired results.

Be mindful of the 21st century reality that working comprises a large portion of our lives. I have always believed that making work as enjoyable, rewarding and productive as possible is the role and responsibility of a focused leader.

Step-5
ENERGIZE OTHERS TO DO THEIR BEST

WHAT TO DO TODAY	WHAT YOU WILL GAIN	WHAT YOU WILL AVOID
Collaboratively create, frequently update and utilize a team member "Empowerment Matrix." The matrix should clearly delineate "empowerment levels" as well as coach your team on how they should respond to unplanned tactical hurdles.	A collaborative method to empower as well as coach your team.	Assuming what levels of empowerment your team members are comfortable accepting.
Develop a simple but relevant set of performance metrics. Measure on a regular basis in a team setting.	The documentation of expectations and the ability of your team to gauge their own performance.	Your team having to wait to know if your entire organization is on-track and meeting goals.
Establish and maintain a formal "recognition program" that rewards excellent achievement.	The "recognition of excellence" as a part of the organizational culture.	Failing to recognize deserving team efforts and team members in a timely manner.

Remember, it's not all about you.

I RECALL DRIVING HOME late one evening after a long day in the office. I was about a year into my first major leadership role where I had the responsibility for multiple business functions. My responsibilities included sales, marketing, engineering, program management, purchasing, quality assurance, manufacturing and finance.

As I reflected on the day's activities, I was somewhat amused by how I had chaired eight meeting in a twelve hour period which involved eight different disciplines and focused on eight different topics. Nowhere in my graduate management studies did I take a class that prepared me for this type of daily routine. I remember saying to myself, *"So, this is what being a leader in a Fortune 100 is all about."*

It's no secret that leaders today must balance many roles and serve multiple audiences --- all while communicating one primary vision. The levels to which you must "compartmentalize" and "juggle" can make you feel like a chameleon. It is also not a secret as to how "being the center" of all of that attention can easily lure you into feeling that all of the contracts won, products produced, services delivered or profits earned are *"all about you."* One of my most admired managers once shared with me that *"A strong leader without a strong team is like a strong horse without a buggy. You can only carry what you can get on your back."*

Yes. The strategy that you provide is important to deciding what to do. The resources (facilities, equipment and capital) you obtain are critical to the process of enabling execution and getting it done. However, there is another --- and perhaps the most important --- piece of the puzzle that is *essential* to winning the contracts, producing the products, delivering the service or generating the profits. It's the *"people"* that your organization hires to get the work done and the values by which they are guided.

"Our people are our most important asset." You most likely have heard these words many times before. Yet, many leaders do not act as if they really believe these words. Over the years, I have grown to embrace these words as a clear expression of a personal value. I have learned that your values form the foundation of your leadership style. Your values permeate the workplace. Your values will largely govern your actions as well as your focus.

As an effective leader, you have an inherent responsibility to both "be the best that you can be" as well as to support efforts that will allow your people to be all that they can be. In doing so, it is important to occasionally remind yourself that, even though you are a critical part of your organization's success, --- it's not all about you.

Step-6
REMEMBER, IT'S NOT ALL ABOUT YOU

WHAT TO DO TODAY	WHAT YOU WILL GAIN	WHAT YOU WILL AVOID
Rotate the chairmanship of your general staff meetings among your direct reports.	The perception of your team that you value their leadership skills and trust their abilities.	Having to select a particular direct report to chair the meeting (each time) in your absence and the perception of "playing favorites."
Encourage your boss to schedule short, "two-down" meetings with your direct reports at least once a year.	The team's recognition that your boss shares your vision and supports you and your organization.	Possible feelings of isolation and uncertainness by your team and organization.
To the extent possible, stay abreast of major events in your team's personal life.	The sense that you care about your team members' well-being outside of the workplace.	Being left out of important internal conversations which may have team building significance.
Consciously use "we" and "our" instead of "I" and "me" in all team communications.	Enhanced perception of valuing teamwork and unity.	Team perception that it's "all about you."

CHAPTER FOUR

SETTING STRATEGIC PARAMETERS

"The essence of strategy is choosing what not to do."

---Michael E. Porter

SETTING STRATEGIC PARAMETERS

YOUR VISION lays out a destination and guides your strategy. It is strategy which links your destination or vision to current reality. Strategy applies to your entire organization and answers the question, "How will we reach our vision, given the current market conditions, economy, competition, regulatory environment, funding, etc.?" Strategy is narrower than vision, but must be broad enough to guide your entire organization.

To achieve your vision, strategy requires action. It is the actions that your team and organization take that will lead to success. However, in those moments of action, having clear strategic direction is crucial for building momentum and staying on the path of success.

Over the years I have found that setting "strategic parameters" for my entire organization is the best way to ensure that the strategic direction I am counting on to win is clear and being properly executed.

Strategic parameters establish the "markers" by which your strategy will be executed. The "markers" are represented by a set of clear and measurable objectives which have immediate relevance and are linked strategically to the success of your entire organization. Encountering a "marker" may require immediate action by you, a particular set of team members or your entire organization.

"Specific markers" are determined by the nature of the specific project or business challenge at hand. Such as "we must complete the first half of the project for a quarter of the allotted funds" or "our product cost must decrease proportionally with competitive price reductions." However, just as important as specific markers are what I call *"psychological and attitudinal markers."* Specific markers set objectives for "what you and your team must do strategically." Psychological and attitudinal markers set objectives for how you and your team will strategically approach or view particular situations in terms of mental psyche and attitude.

Focused Leadership considers setting strategic parameters (specific, psychological and attitudinal) as a critical step in guiding and gauging both the *strategic execution* as well as the *mental presence* required to consistently achieve your organization's goals.

In this chapter you will be introduced to three more steps of the *Focused Leadership* approach to becoming a more effective leader and one of my favorite anecdotes.

ANECDOTE

WHEN A WHISPER IS A ROAR

ON WHAT APPEARED to be a typical mid-August Arizona evening in 1975, the plane landed in Phoenix around 8:30 p.m. It was the end of a long day of activity and travel. It had been an exciting day which originated in Nashville, Tennessee. Around noon of that day, I had graduated summa cum laude from Tennessee State University with a bachelor's degree in Electrical Engineering. I was bubbling with excitement and anticipation.

Within twenty-four hours I would start my first day on the job as a systems engineer at the Honeywell Information Systems Division's Phoenix Computer Operations. After a month of travel to a total of eleven interviews and completing the difficult chore of deciding which of five job offers to accept, it was a great relief to be in Phoenix. I was finally transitioning from college student to an engineering professional.

Even though job offers from IBM, Proctor and Gamble and AT&T contained higher starting salaries, Honeywell's offer included one of only ten coveted positions as a member of the 1975 Class of their Advanced Engineering Program. The Advanced Engineering Program (AEP) was a challenging and unique professional development program. The ten new members that were hired each year were among the top engineering or mathematics graduates from the most highly regarded engineering schools across the country.

The three-year AEP was well-known as a demanding three-prong development program. The program included stimulating, six-month rotating assignments; competitive internal special projects (called 590's and designed to accelerate computer design skills); and mandatory graduate studies at Arizona State University leading to a Master's degree in Engineering or Computer Science. Honeywell decided to maintain the AEP after it acquired the mainframe computer business from General Electric in the early 1970's.

The AEP had a stellar reputation among the Honeywell engineering management staff. AEP members were highly sought after for challenging full time positions upon program completion. To ensure a natural connection with the college and university seniors who would become future program members, Honeywell's senior management would select one member from each graduating AEP class to become the Advanced Engineering Program Manager. The AEP Manager was responsible for managing all aspects of the program with an emphasis on the recruitment of the current year's new class.

Three months into Honeywell's AEP, I was beginning to question the decision I had made for my first job out of college. Without a break, I found myself back into 18-hour days of work and study. But, the work now involved more than part-time labor to support myself through school. The professional work assignments required that I quickly climb steep technical and organizational learning curves. Graduate school and the special 590 projects were as challenging and strenuous as advertised.

However, after completing the first twenty-seven months of the program and a master's degree in Engineering, I was beginning to feel that my choice had been a good one. The rigor and hard work had definitely accelerated and deepened my professional development and significantly enhanced the confidence I had in my skills and abilities. Because I believed I had performed well, both technically and socially in all aspects of the program, I was not entirely surprised when Honeywell's senior management selected me to become the AEP Manager in January 1978.

I spent the last nine-months of my AEP career managing the twenty-nine other program members and leading the company's efforts to identify and recruit the AEP Class of 1978. The AEP Manager's position gave me the opportunity to gain a much broader perspective on how a Fortune 100 company was organized, managed and led.

My office was located on the same floor as the Operation's senior management team and in the heart of the Human Relations Department. Thus, on a daily basis I would bump into the people who established the Phoenix Computer Operation's corporate culture and made the strategic HR, Marketing, Sales, Manufacturing and Engineering decisions.

It was only a few months into this first corporate leadership position that I learned an important lesson about myself and the unintended impact that leadership roles can have on individual team members and the organization as a whole.

The senior manager that I admired and sought the most attention from was, of course, the VP and

Director of Engineering. I felt that if he valued the contribution I was making in the AEP Manager's role, it would naturally enhance my opportunities for future engineering assignments. If, for some reason, he was not pleased with the job I was doing, it might have a negative impact on my career.

I would routinely monitor his office schedule and take advantage of opportunities to meet him in the hallway with confident greetings of "good morning" or "good afternoon." To my surprise, for weeks on end I would meet him in the hallway with a strong greeting and would get no response. Even though my time in the office was fully occupied with AEP management tasks and interview after interview of new hire candidates, I was not able to shake my perception that, for some reason, the Engineering VP was not an Earl Cobb fan.

I soon began losing confidence in myself and the job that I was doing for the company. After a few sleepless nights and a sense of growing anxiety, I finally developed the nerve to confront the perception that seemed to be mounting. I made an appointment to meet with the VP of Engineering. I planned to ask him, point blank, why he was not pleased with me or the job I was doing.

I vividly recall going into his office on a Thursday afternoon expecting a short meeting and the worst. Nevertheless, I was hoping to at least gain some much needed closure.

I found myself leaving his office about an hour later and with an arm on my shoulder. It turned out that for the past several months, he had been struggling with a set of very difficult system design decisions involving the future of the company's computing strategy. The decision making process included the CEO of the Company, the Chief Technology Officer and other corporate level managers. His apparent inattention to me and maybe others in the Phoenix Computer Operation was not meant to indicate any dissatisfaction. It was purely, in his words *"an avoidable oversight and an unintended lapse in leadership focus."*

In September of 1978, with the AEP Class of 1978 safely on board, I graduated from Honeywell's Advanced Engineering Program. That same month, I accepted a full time position as a systems engineer in the Phoenix Computer Operations' I/O Processing Department.

The decision to join the three-year program afforded me the opportunity to gain technical and organizational skills which might have taken five to ten years on a standard engineering career tract. For that, I was truly grateful. With the AEP experience, my professional career rapidly transitioned into senior engineering and future executive management roles.

However, the lesson from the AEP experience that benefitted me the most in my career was the lesson I learned about *myself* and the *role of leadership* following the meeting I had with my Engineering VP back in 1978.

About *myself*, I learned that if you have any questions regarding your relationship with your leadership, you should quickly attempt to gain clarification and a productive resolution. You should not allow speculative perceptions to possibly impact your performance or derail career opportunities.

About the *role of leadership*, I learned that when you become a leader, "your whisper becomes a roar." As a leader, your team members --- and the organization as a whole --- listen attentively to your every word. Correspondingly, they will inevitably perceive the lack of communication for a prolonged period of time as a negative. An *avoidable oversight and an unintended lapse in leadership focus* can sometimes have unintended and, in many cases, damaging organizational impact. To those under a leader's command --- *a whisper is a roar.*

"Leaders establish the vision for the future and set the strategy for getting there."

---John P. Kotter

Set a course lined with short-term successes.

YOU CANNOT EXPECT your team to know or understand every aspect of the operational strategy required to fulfill your vision. It is up to you, as the leader, to set the proper course and provide the strategic bearings for getting from here to there.

In addition to regularly articulating their vision, effective leaders also spend time illustrating how best to strategically achieve the goals, overcome the challenges and reach the vision. At times, leaders must clearly explain a team member's strategic role in fulfilling the vision and meeting the challenges. This type of "on-going" direction and coaching is not only informational but is also inspirational.

Occasionally, based on the makeup of your team, it may be necessary to coach team members that are in key operational roles. These team members must maintain the mindset required to read strategic "markers" placed in operational environments. Strategic thinking is by nature not inherent in all individuals and may differ in degree among team members. The proper strategic mindset provides your team with the ability to come up with all the best possible solutions for various scenarios. The goal is to have them respond to internal or external factors in a manner consistent with the strategy required to reach your vision. Thinking strategically is also an effective and useful way to create short-term and long-term options which might result in more successful solutions.

Experience over the years has taught me that, along with strategic direction, your team and organization also need to feel that they are making progress toward reaching your vision. A sense of progress is important in order to maintain the passion that your vision provided from the outset. I have found that setting a strategic course lined with short-term successes is an effective and powerful way to provide your team with a true sense of accomplishment.

Short-term successes seem to have the same effect on our psyche and sense of progress as do long-term successes and major accomplishments. Researchers have determined that one of best ways for people to see progress is through short-term successes. Short-term successes seem to set in motion the wheels of motivation, productivity and passion. However, you must remember that short-term successes are only effective if they are visible to the entire team and the victory is closely related to the ultimate goal.

Therefore, to become a more effective leader, you should supplement your vision with "on-going" strategic direction; discretionary coaching on strategic thinking; and a course lined with short-term successes.

Step-7
SET A COURSE LINED WITH SHORT-TERM SUCCESSES

WHAT TO DO TODAY	WHAT YOU WILL GAIN	WHAT YOU WILL AVOID
Supplement your vision with "on-going" strategic direction.	Team will stay on course and have the strategic bearings required to get from here to there.	Your organization missing critical strategic goals due to lack of "big picture" clarity.
Provide discretionary coaching on strategic thinking.	The strategic mind-set your critical team members need to recognize and act upon key strategic markers.	Risk of team not recognizing or acting upon key strategic markers.
Target short-term successes that are visible to your entire organization.	A team with a sense of making progress toward reaching the organization's vision. A more motivated, productive and passionate team.	A discouraged and less motivated team due to a sense of not making progress.
Ensure that short-term successes are achievable and linked to the ultimate goal.	Obtainment of short-term success per plan and a true sense of progress.	Possible failure to obtain the short-term success, as planned, and/or lack of connection to goal.

Have the courage to make the right decisions.

ONE OF MY FAVORITE leadership quotes is one that is attributed to Winston Churchill. It states, *"Courage is what it takes to stand up and speak; courage is also what it takes to sit down and listen."*

Throughout my career I have been both a practitioner and student of leadership. I have read almost every book on leadership that I have been able to get my hands on. Most of the contemporary literature on leadership focuses on leadership styles, characteristics, principles, traits, models, etc. Much of the literature offers a great deal of historical insight, comparisons and advice. However, what I have found to be most intriguing is how the virtue of "courage" seems to be omnipresent. Aristotle once called courage the first virtue and alluded to the fact that courage is the virtue which makes all of the other virtues possible.

I believe that in addition to being the most important human virtue, when it comes to organizational performance and success --- courage is also the most important virtue of an effective leader.

The reason I have been such a fan of the Winston Churchill quote mentioned above is that I have learned that in the context of leadership, courage is both a "verb" and a "conjunction." It takes a certain brand of courage to execute both the "gives" and the "takes" required to get the best results for the entire organization. Effective team and organizational leadership is about being able to synergistically blend talent and get the most out of diverse human experiences. In order to make this approach to leadership work for everyone involved, you must possess the brand of "courage" that allows you to not only fearlessly *"stand up and speak"* but to also fearlessly *"sit down and listen."*

In addition, *Focused Leadership* is characterized by an intense focus on decision making which complements this brand of courage. As leaders, we are not strangers to decision making. However, we all find ourselves faced with the need to make a decision that is right for our team but challenging for others (and maybe ourselves) to swallow. I can recall scores of decisions I have made over my career which fall into this category. They all, at the time, seemed to take on the dimensions of "life or death" decisions. However, in hindsight, I recall that every decision that landed "on the side of the team as a whole" turned out to be the right decision.

As a part of your effort to become a more effective leader, you should strive to have the brand of courage required to make decisions that are best for your team and your organization's success.

Step-8
HAVE THE COURAGE TO MAKE THE RIGHT DECISIONS

WHAT TO DO TODAY	WHAT YOU WILL GAIN	WHAT YOU WILL AVOID
Identify the objective to be achieved by each decision.	Valuable insight into other possible ways to get the same result.	Making a difficult decision to achieve an objective that could be reached in another manner.
Minimize choices associated with each decision by setting strategic guidelines.	The assurance that your decision is in alignment with your organization's strategy for success.	Making a decision which is contrary to your organization's overall strategy.
Attempt to isolate personal emotions from the decision making process.	More objective decisions.	Personal partiality which may not be in the best interest of the organization.
Increase the involvement of others.	Additional perspectives and expertise injected into the decision making process.	Isolated, short-sighted decisions.

Insist on accountability and respect from all.

CREATING a greater accountability at every level of your organization is a means to gaining both organizational improvement and building an organization of mutual respect. When you fail to hold others accountable, you reap the consequences --- some obvious and some not so obvious.

Accountability is the willingness and interest to assume responsibility for one's work and actions. It occurs only when team members accept full ownership of the results of their work. Without accountability, your organization is incapable of achieving and sustaining its best performance.

In leading high performance organizations, I have always made a concerted effort to utilize personal and team accountability to drive the execution of strategy and the accomplishment of organizational goals. Although the prospect of instilling accountability throughout an entire organization can seem daunting, I have found that each team member within an organization has the capability, if called upon, to contribute to building personal and team accountability. However, accountability is not something you can make people do. It has to be chosen, accepted and agreed upon by all the members within your organization. Your team must "buy in" to being accountable and responsible.

Also as a leader, it is vital that the people you are leading have respect for you. If you have their respect, they will work harder and longer to help you reach your vision.

Mutual respect is one of many values that most organizations seek to institutionalize. Like all values, it cannot be legislated or regulated into existence. However, it can be learned and it can be coached. It must also be demonstrated by you as the team's leader.

From an organizational context, a team's respect is not something handed to you when you take on a new leadership role. It is an essential leadership quality that you must build and earn over time. I have learned that if you know what you want, maintain a positive attitude, make yourself available and value team member differences, you can accelerate the process.

Although there is no sure method for gaining respect in a leadership role or instilling accountability instantly within an organization, as the team's leader you should still insist on accountability and respect from all. Then, you should aggressively establish and embrace a workplace environment which will provide nourishment to both.

Step-9
INSIST ON ACCOUNTABILITY AND RESPECT FROM ALL

WHAT TO DO TODAY	WHAT YOU WILL GAIN	WHAT YOU WILL AVOID
Know what you want.	The respect of your team. It is difficult to respect someone who is not sure what he or she wants.	Loss of team member respect and accountability.
Develop and train your team to feel accountable for their actions.	Assurance that team members are aware of what's expected and have insight into what to improve.	Team member "push-back" due to lack of training and unclear expectations.
Earn the trust and respect of the people you are leading.	The foundation for developing productive relationships.	The inability to establish essential elements required to build critical relationships.
Avoid showing favoritism toward specific team members.	Trust and accountability of the entire team.	Your team's perception that you do not value everyone's contribution.

CHAPTER FIVE

"Losers live in the past. Winners learn from the past and enjoy working in the present toward the future."

---Denis Waitley

LEADING AND WINNING

WHEN I DECIDED to leave my Systems Engineering position at Honeywell in 1979 and join Motorola as a Program Manager, I was well aware that I was transitioning into my leadership career. Starting out, I found myself chasing down every opportunity to shine. I wanted to be successful and I wanted to quickly demonstrate that I had the stuff required to be an effective leader in a Fortune 100 company. The Program Management role was my chance to become a leader and move into the senior management ranks. That day eventually came in 1986 when I became the Director of Program Management with the ELDEC Corporation. Along with this new responsibility came the need to create winning teams in order to produce the desired results.

As a young manager, I often found myself getting somewhat upset when my ideas were not listened to or my directions were not followed. I recall trying to get people to listen to me and if they did not, they were labeled as non-team players. I must confess that I did everything in my power to remove them from my group. However, since that time, I have learned a lot about what an effective leader is and what an effective leader does, in order to build trust and develop winning teams.

One invaluable and fundamental lesson regarding leadership that I have learned over the years is how to develop a "winning mindset."

Have you ever wondered why some people just seem to be better at everything? They seem to handle stress better, operate with more mental clarity, have that air of confidence and know exactly what they want. When you look at them, they don't appear to be any smarter, more talented or better in any way than you. Yet, they get results. Well, that is what a winning mindset is all about.

The revelation that contributed to galvanizing my ability to establish and maintain a winning mindset was the realization that *our thoughts* are what dictate our moods, our emotions, our body language and ultimately our ability to perform. Once I began to *first* approach every leadership challenge *mentally*, I began to experience what it is like to consistently lead and win.

What many young and not so young leaders forget is that the origin of our thoughts is not random. When we learn to control our thoughts, we gain the ability to ensure that we perform with a feeling of self-confidence. The most effective leaders have a strong connection with their inner thoughts.

The *Focus Management* approach to leading and winning emphasizes the training of your inner thoughts to always work in your favor.

ANECDOTE

IN THE EYE OF A HURRICANE

I WAS SUDDENLY awakened from a catnap by the rocking of the small jet as we prepared to land at the Daytona Beach International airport. It was a stormy Sunday evening in February 1998. I was on board the Reynolds and Reynolds Company's corporate jet with Dave Holmes, who was President and CEO of Reynolds and Reynolds at the time. We were completing a flight from San Francisco to Daytona Beach, Florida. Daytona Beach was our last stop on a five-day business trip.

Dave and I left the Reynolds and Reynolds Headquarters in Dayton, Ohio on Thursday to spend the weekend at the National Automobile Dealers Association (NADA) Convention in San Francisco. I had just completed my eighth month with the company as Vice President of Operations for the Healthcare Systems Division. As we were scheduling the trip, I suggested to Dave that we should stop by Daytona Beach on our way back to Dayton. It would be a good opportunity for him to visit our newest Healthcare Systems Division business acquisition.

I joined the Reynolds and Reynolds Company and its Healthcare Systems Division (HSD) in July of 1997. HSD was the newest Division of the 100-year-old management services company. Dave Holmes became Reynolds and Reynolds President and CEO about eight years earlier and HSD was his brain-child. HSD was into its fourth year of business operations.

As Vice President of Operations, I was responsible for leading all of HSD's business operations and customer support activity. The Operations Unit was comprised of four Customer Support Centers located in Portland, San Diego, Birmingham and Daytona Beach. Each Support Center included a systems installation team, a field services team, a software development & maintenance team, a program management team and a customer service hotline. Each Center was established as the result of Reynolds and Reynolds' acquisition of small healthcare practice management software companies. The business acquisitions were the cornerstone of the company's HSD growth strategy.

Each Center supported a unique computer technology, custom software and a specific customer base. Reynolds and Reynolds Healthcare Systems customers included hospitals, physician offices and practice management service providers.

The custom software supported the day-to-day operations and allowed users to capture patient demographics, schedule appointments, maintain lists of insurance payers, perform billing tasks and generate reports.

When I joined Reynolds and Reynolds in 1997, the Portland, San Diego and Birmingham business acquisitions were completed. The Customer Support Centers were in various stages of operational and organizational overhaul. However, I was confidently on board and actively involved in the acquisition of the Daytona Beach software company. This particular company was the smallest that Reynolds and Reynolds had acquired to date. But, the owner had managed to establish it as a leader in the Southeastern United States for the hospital-based Radiology market segment. It was considered a prize acquisition.

The Reynolds and Reynolds Company had a long and successful history of developing and marketing business management support systems. The company had pioneered and was a long-time market leader in the automobile dealer market. Its custom software enabled business efficiencies throughout the dealership process. However, with the move into the ultra-competitive healthcare systems business, the Reynolds and Reynolds senior management team realized the need to update the company's operations management skills as well as to enhance the executive leadership team's talent in this critical arena.

I recognized during my initial discussions and the subsequent recruitment process why Reynolds and Reynolds was particularly interested in my background and skill-set. Motorola was an industry leader in implementing Six Sigma and Total Quality Management (TQM) techniques in the United States at the time. I had a proven track record of effectively utilizing both techniques in my role as Motorola's Vice President of Radio Systems Operations.

Therefore, as I started my new leadership role within Reynolds and Reynolds, I moved purposefully to ensure that the operational overhauls within all of the new HSD Customer Support Centers would meet senior management's expectations.

As the plane rolled down the runway and pulled into the gate at Daytona Beach International, I was rehearsing my introduction of Dave to my Daytona Customer Support Center team. I had asked my team managers to walk Dave through the new operation management processes we had worked diligently to establish over the past six months. I knew that the results-to-date could only be viewed as early trends. However, based on the results presented to me during the previous week's operations reviews, I felt that Dave would be impressed with where we were heading.

I was somewhat concerned with what Dave might hear from the Daytona management team regarding their first six-months as a Reynolds and Reynolds business unit. I was also curious as to what he might hear from them regarding my first six months as their leader.

I purposely kept the Daytona management team in tack after the acquisition. This was somewhat unusual and not consistent with the moves I had to make within the other three Customer Support Centers. Customer and service issues inherited from the previous owners required that I replace, at least, the General Managers at the other locations. Although I found the Daytona team understaffed and lacking in process discipline, all of their customers loved them. There were no major customer issues.

The Daytona General Manager was young, but smart and seemed open to leading his team through the changes required to achieve the new Reynolds and Reynolds customer satisfaction targets.

However, due to the timing of the acquisition and the need for HSD to aggressively grow the "hospital-based" business, I had to set some aggressive targets for the Daytona Customer Support Center.

The targets required everyone in the support center to climb some steep learning curves. They would have to learn new processes and customer management techniques. I personally spent several weeks on-site with the Daytona Call Center Manager and her team. Together, we crafted a triaging technique that would reduce the response time associated with all levels of customer support requests.

I insisted that the General Manager meet daily with the entire Support Center team to discuss and resolve all issues as soon as possible. I knew that open, honest communications between the team members and the local leadership team was essential during this transition. I also assisted in the development of performance metrics for all Support Center departments. When I began my evaluation of the Daytona team based on the new metrics shortly after their implementation, I was concerned that I might have a mutiny on my hands. Fortunately the team stood up and swiftly accepted the change. My experience told me that this kind of aggressive, yet caring "focus" now, would pay off in the long run.

Dave and I arrived at the Daytona Support Center around 8:00 a.m. on Monday morning. Everyone was in place and we moved through all of the planned tours, briefings, metric reviews and lunch without a hitch. Based on Dave's comments, I felt that he was pleased with what he found at the new Daytona Beach location. He shared with me that all of his discussions with the Daytona management team had gone well. Of course, this was a welcomed relief.

Prior to closing out the day, I asked Dave to speak briefly to the entire Daytona team. We were all gathered in a large meeting room near the call center. Dave took about ten minutes to congratulate the entire team on how quickly they had transitioned to the Reynolds and Reynolds way of doing things. He asked them to keep up the good work and promised to visit the location again in the near future to review the team's progress.

As we were about to leave the room, the Daytona General Manager stepped up front with what looked like a picture wrapped in brown paper. He congratulated his team not only on how well they had handled Dave's visit but also how well they managed the facility shutdown a few weeks earlier when a hurricane (named "Earl") had passed along the Daytona Beach coast.

Then, he opened the package to reveal a colorful aerial photo of the actual hurricane taken by a weather.com satellite. Across the top of the picture were the words, "Hurricane Earl."

He asked me to come to the front. On behalf of the entire Daytona team, he passionately shared with me, for the first time, how proud they were to work for me and how much they valued my leadership. He stated that, initially, the team was not so appreciative and was beginning to feel as if they were in the eye of a "Reynolds and Reynolds" hurricane. But, as they began to see the results of the changes, they also began to enjoy their jobs even more. He thanked me for my passion and my focused leadership. At that time, he presented me the photo of "Hurricane Earl."

As the Reynolds and Reynolds corporate jet lifted off and headed back to Ohio early that evening, Dave leaned back and thanked me for what I had done in such a short time in Daytona Beach. I leaned back and could only think of the Daytona Support Center team and how their simple expression of gratitude had permanently etched a lasting memory in my heart.

Persist with purpose, passion and focus.

PERSISTENCE, purpose, passion and focus are fundamental characteristics of effective leaders. Gaining persistence requires determination and a mindset. Persistence in leadership is somewhat analogous to running a marathon. To run a successful marathon you have to spend ample time preparing. The time you spend and what you do leading up to the race will determine how well you perform in the race.

I believe that the traditional textbook definitions of a leader's purpose, such as maximizing employee performance, are old news. In today's fast-paced world of the Internet, social media and global competitiveness, a leader's purpose is to ensure that "new futures" are created as rapidly as external markets evolve.

Also, as a leader, your passion and attitude are contagious and uplifting. They set the mood for everyone around you. The same goes for your focus. It you have a "laser" focus and a mindset to win, so will your team. Leadership is simple, but is not easy. One of the factors that separate effective leaders from others is their ability to focus their attention, not just on dealing with crises, but on creating and executing ideas to move the organization forward.

If you persist with purpose, passion and focus in everything you do --- you will consistently lead and win.

Step-10
PERSIST WITH PURPOSE, PASSION AND FOCUS

WHAT TO DO TODAY	WHAT YOU WILL GAIN	WHAT YOU WILL AVOID
Find your voice. Develop a controlled, relaxed and clear voice.	The confidence associated with a controlled, relaxed and clear voice.	Sounding tentative and unsure.
Have a winning routine. Develop a routine that you can associate to feeling great and being ready to perform.	The perception of always being ready, passionate and possessing a positive attitude.	The perception of being moody and not always yourself.
Run the movie. Create a clear and vivid image in your mind --- complete with sights, sounds and emotions of what's required for each "performance."	The perception of being focused and "in the moment."	Being viewed as unfocused and not passionate about your message.
Walk the walk. Assume the body language and attitude of a confident leader.	Always being viewed as "the confident person" that you are.	Not being viewed as consistently confident.

"Our thoughts create our reality – where we put our focus is the direction we tend to go."

---Peter McWilliams

AUTHOR'S NOTE

A man was struggling to cut down enough trees to build a fence.

An old farmer came by, watched for a while, then quietly said, "Saw's kind of dull, isn't it?"

"I reckon," said the fence builder.

"Hadn't ya better sharpen it?," asked the old farmer.

The fence builder replied, "Maybe later. I can't stop now --- I got all these trees to cut down."

--- From Mackenzie (1990). The Time Trap. New York: AMACOM, pg. 11

Moral of the Story: If you take time to sharpen your leadership skills, the task will not be so hard.

Now that you have read *Focused Leadership* for the first time, you might be asking yourself, "Where do I go from here?"

Well…it's really up to you. As noted in the moral of the little story above, you have a decision to make.

- If any of the thirty-nine ideas presented as things that *"you can do today"* to become a more effective leader can be integrated into your current leadership approach and you are comfortable with your management skill-set to fully implement them … then go for it. Chances are you will never regret that you did.

- If some of the thirty-nine ideas presented as actions can enhance your current leadership approach but you are not comfortable with your current management skill-set to fully implement them (such as scenario planning, strategic planning, employee coaching, performance metric development, etc.), then lay out a plan to expand your management skill-set.

- If some of the thirty-nine ideas presented as actions can enhance your current leadership approach but now is not a "good time" to make a change or fully implement them, then keep them in mind until the right time comes along.

However, by all means, keep a copy of *Focused Leadership* close at hand. In leadership development, as in all areas of professional growth, you must set objectives, develop a realistic action plan and execute the plan to its fullest in order to achieve your maximum success. I believe that *Focused Leadership* and the "10-Step Approach to Leading and Winning" can uniquely assist you in this process.

Above all, remember that life is too short to put off for tomorrow, what you can do today.

As a personal note --- make sure you hug your family daily and seek every opportunity to *smell the roses*.

ABOUT THE AUTHOR

ERVIN (EARL) COBB

Earl Cobb is an American "rags-to-riches" success story. Through his hard work, dedication and faith, Earl has forged an accomplished career as a systems engineer, program manager, corporate executive and a gifted entrepreneur.

Since 2009, Earl has been the CEO and Managing Partner of Richer Life, LLC --- a Media, Trade Book Publishing and Professional Services company, headquartered in Phoenix, Arizona.

He has enjoyed over thirty years of success within Fortune 100, Mid-Market and Venture companies including *Honeywell, Inc.*, *Motorola, Inc.*, the *Reynolds and Reynolds Company* and *Wells Fargo Bank*. He is the former President, COO and CEO of *MedContrax, Inc.*

Earl earned a Bachelor of Science degree, with honors, in Electrical Engineering from Tennessee State University and graduated from Arizona State University with the degree of Master of Science in Engineering.

He is a former Adjunct Professor of Management at the Keller Graduate School of Management of DeVry University and has completed graduate studies at Stanford University's Graduate School of Business, the Sloan School of Management at MIT and the Center for Creative Leadership.

Earl has been honored with numerous national awards for professional achievement including the 1995 Black Engineer of the Year Award.

Earl and his wife, Dr. Charlotte Grant-Cobb, have authored four books together, *Living a Richer Life: Getting the Most out of Life's Gifts and Circumstances*, *Navigating the Life Enrichment Model*™, *Pillow Talk Consciousness: Intimate Reflections on America's 100 Most Interesting Thoughts and Suspicions* and *God's Goodness and Our Mindfulness*.

Earl's second book on leadership titled, *The Leadership Advantage: Do More. Lead More. Earn More.* is scheduled to be released in 2015.

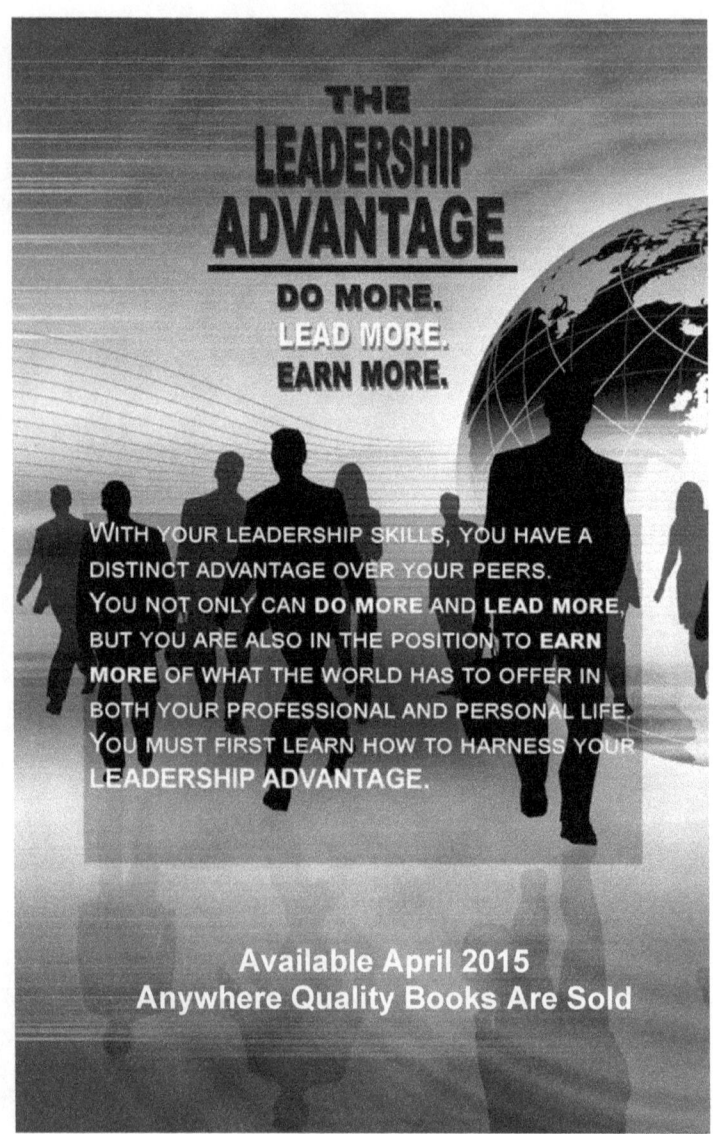

"No life ever grows great until it is focused, dedicated and disciplined."
---Unknown Author

╬RICHER Press
An Imprint of Richer Life, LLC

RICHER Press is a full service, specialty Trade publisher whose sole goal is to *shape thoughts and change lives for the better*. All of the books, eBooks and digital media we publish, distribute and market embrace our commitment to help maximize opportunities for personal growth and professional achievement.

To learn more visit
www.richerlifellc.com.

www.ingramcontent.com/pod-product-compliance
Lightning Source LLC
Chambersburg PA
CBHW051808040426
42446CB00007B/580